COBRA

SHELBY AMERICAN ORIGINAL ARCHIVES 1962–1965

DAVE FRIEDMAN

MOTORBOOKS
INTERNATIONAL

This edition published in 2002 by Motorbooks International, an imprint of MBI Publishing Company, Galtier Plaza, Suite 200, 380 Jackson Street, St. Paul, MN 55101-3885 USA

Motorbooks International titles are also available at discounts in bulk quantity for industrial or sales-promotional use. For details write to Special Sales Manager at Motorbooks International Wholesalers & Distributors, Galtier Plaza, Suite 200, 380 Jackson Street, St. Paul, MN 55101-3885 USA.

Library of Congress Cataloging-in-Publication Data Available

ISBN 0-7603-1368-7

On the front cover: This Cobra is running ahead of the pack at Daytona 1964. *Pete Biro*

On the frontispiece: Carroll Shelby sits behind the wheel of a Cobra in this promotional photograph taken in 1963 and distributed by Shelby American, Inc. *Pete Biro*

On the title page: Besides being one of the best looking cars on the track, the Shelby Cobra also packs incredible speed as shown here at Sebring 1964. *Pete Biro*

On the back cover, top: Dan Gurney pilots a Cobra at Daytona in 1964. *Pete Biro.*
Bottom: This Cobra, the crowd favorite, heads into the home stretch at Sebring in 1964. *Pete Biro*

Printed in Hong Kong

Contents

Acknowledgments

I would like to thank Carroll Shelby and Pete Brock who believed in me from the beginning. It was Pete who convinced Carroll to hire me in the first place. Deke Houlgate, Shelby American's original, public relations man, believed in me and always encouraged me to achieve my best and not compromise.

As always, Tim Parker, Michael Dregni, and the staff at Motorbooks International have been wonderful. Their patience, dedication, and encouragement have been first class.

A number of other people have contributed to this book in various ways. Jack Sears, John Willment, Wally Peat, Sherry MacDonald, Ed Leslie, Bob Holbert, and Allen Grant shared their memories with me. Carol and Katy Christy allowed me to quote from their late father's writings. Bernard Cahier, Kathy Agar at LAT, and Alexis Callier supplied some additional photographs.

Sherry MacDonald, Allen Grant, Tom Warth, and Carroll Shelby have joined the author and loaned much of their personal memorabilia to be photographed for this book. To them a huge thank you for sharing it with the readers.

Maggie Logan-Moore photographed all of the memorabilia and contributed many good ideas and suggestions. She also helped with the research, picture selection, and darkroom work.

Susan, the lady in my life, lived those Shelby years with me and knew many of the people involved and also attended many of the races with me. Her biggest complaint at the time was that when she went to the races with me, that she never saw me.

Maggie and Susan corrected my terrible grammar, spelling, and sentence structure. Between the two of them, they made it look as if I really knew what I was doing.

All dates, race facts, and Shelby American dates are from official company records, press releases, official race results, and entry sheets. Background sources include *AutoSport*, *MotorSport*, *Sports Car Graphic*, *Road & Track*, and *Automobile Year*. Quotes are from recorded and written interviews, press releases, or filmed interviews, most of which were done specifically for this book in 1991–1993.

Foreword

When we began building the Cobra in 1962, we had no idea what we were starting. Who knew that it would grow into the legend that it has today? Hell, I just thought we were building a few production cars to help finance our racing. Racing is what we were all about and that's what we did best.

We had many great people at Shelby American, mechanics, drivers, and support staff, and they performed incredible tasks under the most adverse conditions. I think we had the finest group of people ever gathered together in one small company. We were very close, all friends, and most of us still stay in touch today. Our Venice operations was special, and when we moved to the airport in 1965, the true spirit of Shelby American died and we lost a lot of good people.

Dave Friedman came to Shelby American on the recommendation of Pete Brock. Though none of us knew it at the time, Dave's photographs would document our history and he would preserve it through his many books and magazine contributions.

He is the keeper of the flame.

Carroll Shelby
January 1994

Preface

I worked at Shelby American, Inc., during the years 1962–1965 as the company and race team photographer. I shot production pictures, advertising photos, Carroll Shelby School of High Performance Driving pictures, Goodyear tire pictures, progress photos of ongoing projects, the official homologation photos, racing pictures, and more. The thousands of color and black and white negatives and color transparencies in my files are the closet thing to an official Shelby American archive.

This book is not about words, it's about pictures. Most of the words have already been written, many times, by people far more qualified then I. What I am hoping to do here is present many of the photographs that I took while at Shelby American that have not been previously published or have not been published in many years. I think I have accomplished that.

Unfortunately I did not shoot much color film during that period; I wish, now, that I had shot more. Shelby American, however, had little use for it at the time. Most of our requirements for ads, press material, and magazine photos were all black and white.

The homologation photography was an important part of my work and it was a job that allowed me to work closely with Ken Miles. I also spent a lot of time doing public relations photography and press kits for Deke Houlgate, our first, and best, public relations man. In addition, I worked closely with Pete Brock on many of his projects.

The Shelby team, as great as it was, was supported by many industrious privateers—individuals and teams. The phenomenal British teams of John Willment, Chequered Flag, and Tommy Atkins scored many victories with drivers such as Jack Sears, Frank Gardner, Bob Olthoff, Roger Mac, and Roy Salvadori. American teams like Essex Wire and drivers of the caliber of Bob Johnson, Tom Payne, Bobby Brown, Skip Scott, Dick Thompson, and Charlie Parsons also scored numerous victories.

Working with the people in the race shop, testing at Riverside, and going to the races was, of course, the major part of my job. It was a dream come true for a young photographer and I eagerly took advantage of every opportunity. To be around the talent that we had in our shop and on the racetrack inspired me to better myself at my craft and do some of my best work.

Some of the best friends I ever had were my teammates at that time, and I still see many of them today. We were all young and having the time of our lives. I wouldn't have traded that experience for anything that I've done before or since.

Looking back, working at Shelby American was one of the greatest experiences of my life. My job there gave me a great deal of independence. I also learned a lot about professionalism and dedication to a project that I have never forgotten. The fact that I expect as much from those around me as I give myself was also learned at Shelby American. Having had a chance to walk with legends and be a participant on one of the greatest racing teams ever is a part of my life I will cherish forever.

This book is dedicated to all of the Shelby American employees who called Princeton Street our home and called each other friend.

Dave Friedman
January 1994

Photo passes and arm bands for races that Shelby American participated in during the 1963, 1964, and 1965 seasons.

Left
Dave Friedman and Cobra coupe, 1964
Everyone wanted to stand alongside the Cobra coupe and have their picture taken—including myself.

BUY IT !......OR WATCH IT GO BY !

SHELBY AC/COBRA POWERED BY FORD

Chapter 1

1962

The Shelby Cobra Is Born

Legend has it that Shelby American was born at Lance Reventlow's famous ex-Scarab shop at 1042 Princeton Drive in Venice, California, in mid-1962. The truth of the matter is that the company originated in the back of hot rodder Dean Moon's shop in Santa Fe Springs, California, in February 1962, and didn't move to Venice until June 1962.

The story of how Carroll Shelby formed Shelby American has been told so many times that it has become part of automotive mythology. Shelby heard that AC Cars of Surrey, England, was ending production of its Bristol sports car. Inspired by the all-American horsepower available from

Shelby Logo, 1962
The Shelby name was hand painted on the nose of the prototype as the name "Cobra" had not yet been thought up. Note the holes were the AC badge had been bolted on.

Shelby Cobra Badge, 1962
The first Cobra badge installed at Shelby American on the 260 series cars. Note the name included, at that time, the AC logo.

First Cobra Brochure, 1962
Cobra brochure with a black and white photograph of the first car, chassis number CSX2000, pictured at a golf course near Dean Moon's shop and modeled by Carroll Shelby's secretary wearing a tiara and gloves for the occasion. The car's bodywork had yet to be painted when these publicity photos were shot so we buffed out the aluminum to a high luster with steel wool so it would shine in the sun. *Tom Warth Collection*

Chevrolet's small-block V-8, he proposed marrying the two into a California-bred hot rod. Chevrolet said no, so Shelby talked Ford into the deal. The rest is history.

Like Enzo Ferrari before him, Carroll Shelby lived to race, and the production and sale of street cars was a means to go racing. "We built production cars so we could go racing," was Carroll Shelby's well-documented quote and it pretty well summed up the attitude that prevailed at Shelby American.

Although many of us considered the production side of our company as secondary, we must remember that this part of the company turned out 1,011 Cobras between February 1962 and the last 427 Cobra, which rolled off the production line in March 1967.

The production division helped create a street legend that has grown to epic proportions through the years.

Building the First Cobra
Inside AC Cars of England

The prototype Cobra was built at AC Cars in Thames Ditton, Surrey, England, in January 1962. The prototype was based on AC chassis number CSX2000.

AC mechanics fitted the prototype with a 221ci Ford V-8 engine for testing and evaluation. After some chassis modifications, the prototype chassis—with bodywork but less engine and transmission—was air freighted on February 2, 1962, to Carroll Shelby in Los Angeles.

AC Cars Factory, 1962
AC Cars' Dennis Hurlock supervises the installation of the Ford 221ci engine into the first Cobra chassis, CSX2000. This car was sent via air freight to the United States minus the engine and transmission in early February.

Right
AC Cars Factory, 1962
The first Cobra, chassis number CSX2000, under construction at the AC Cars plant in early January 1962. The engine shown here was a 221ci Ford V-8 engine used for placing the motor mounts, steering, and so on, as well as for early testing by AC. The name Cobra had not yet been conceived at this time.

California Sports Car
At Work in Dean Moon's Hot Rod Shop

When the prototype CSX2000 chassis arrived in the United States by air, it was rushed to Dean Moon's shop in Santa Fe Springs, California. Our team lowered in a 260ci V-8 Ford engine connected to a four-speed Borg-Warner transmission. Installing the new engine took less then eight hours, and the first car was ready for a dash around the block to see how it worked.

Dean Moon Shop, 1962
The first Cobra nearing completion. The AC Cars air freight tag was still taped to the trunk lid at this point. Note the worker wearing the famous Moon eyes t-shirt.

Right
Dean Moon Shop, 1962
The first 260ci engine, XHP-260-1, is installed in the first production Cobra. The mechanic in the foreground is getting ready to install the fuel lines while the other workers prepare to re-install the interior. The AC badge on the front of the car was soon removed.

Dean Moon Shop, 1962
With its top up and all shipping tags removed, the car is about ready for its first start up and an initial road test by Carroll Shelby and Dean Moon. The man at the front of the car is completing the removal of the AC badge and the painting of Shelby's name on the hood.

Letting the Cobra Loose
The First Road Tests

Within hours of completion, John Christy, editor of *Sports Car Graphic*, went Corvette hunting with the unpainted prototype Cobra. He found no takers.

By May 1962, the magazine tests were on the newsstands, already calling the Cobra's acceleration "explosive." These early reviews sparked interest everywhere and orders started coming in.

By June 1962, production was proceeding—but slowly as numerous chassis modifications had to be made.

Publicity Photo, 1962
The first car was originally painted a brilliant pearlescent yellow by master hot-rod and custom-car paint whiz Dean Jeffries. It was soon repainted in a variety of different colors to make the magazines think there were more Cobras pouring forth from the factory when actually we only had the prototype working overtime.

Dashboard, 1962
The incomplete dashboard of the first Cobra at the time of the initial road test. Who needed a speedometer anyway?

Right
Publicity Photo, 1962
We took the completed car out to a golf course near Dean Moon's shop for its first batch of publicity photographs in mid-1962. Here, Carroll Shelby sat behind the steering wheel while his secretary, dressed in tiara and gloves, stood alongside.

Road Test, 1962
John Christy, editor of *Sports Car Graphic* and one of the Cobra godfathers, takes to the streets of Los Angeles hours after the completion of CSX2000 in search of Corvettes. He found no takers. Christy described his first sight of the newly completed Cobra: "At first glance it was an unpainted AC Bristol with a longer nose. The net visual effect was to transform what had heretofore been very desirable property into a device that had grown hair in large bundles. The thing hadn't even been fired up and yet it seemed to sit there growling, mashing its teeth, and swishing its tail. Not even Shelby knew what he had by the tail at that moment; about all anyone could tell at that point was that whatever it was, it was *mean*."

Early Cobra Brochures
Selling Shelby American

Throughout the birth of the first production Shelby Cobras, I shot photographs of the cars during construction, while testing, racing, and more. In the coming months, these photos went to make up the early Shelby American brochures for the Cobra.

Left
The AC Cobra fitted with an AC badge on the front hood. *Tom Warth Collection*

Below
An early English AC brochure for the Cobra with mention of the Ford and Shelby connection reserved for page 3. *Tom Warth Collection*

SHELBY AC COBRA
POWERED BY FORD

An early Cobra 260ci sales brochure. The title of the car paid due homage to
all of its creators: Shelby AC Cobra Powered by Ford.

Building the First Racer
Bill Krause's 260ci Snake

In November 1962, the 260ci Cobra was homologated by the Fédération Internationale de l'Automobile (FIA) with only eight cars built instead of the 100 required. How did we get FIA homologation approval? It was an old game; everyone was playing and everyone was guilty.

Just as Ferrari had done with the 250 GTO, Shelby promised the FIA that we would build the remaining cars to bring production to 100. We would eventually reach 100, but it took time—and by that point the Cobra had already scored some impressive victories. Ferrari's 250 GTO never reached 100, of course, and for that Ferrari later had problems with its GTO mid-engined derivative, the 250 LM. It was all a game of who was the best at pulling the wool over the other's eyes.

It is interesting to note that the homologation papers for the later 289ci version certified that 100 cars had been built by November 30, 1962. To my recollection, none of these 289 cars were built until January 1963. So whereas we had homologated the 260 Cobra with only eight cars, we homologated the 289 with no cars.

Riverside Endurance Race, 1962
Carroll Shelby, right, and an Autolite engineer check the spark plugs prior to the start of the three-hour endurance race at Riverside.

Cobra Race Engine, 1962
The first 260ci V-8 racing engine as used in the first racing Cobra was not much different from the production 260ci engine. The race engine was modified with higher compression and a Spalding Flamethrower ignition. Here was engine number XHP-260-8 fitted to chassis CSX2002 prior to the Riverside debut.

Cobra Homologation Lineup, 1962
The eight existing Cobras—seven production cars and one race car (at far end, with rollbar)—at the time of our filing for homologation. Technically there were supposed to be 100 finished cars but promises were made that the other ninety-two were in preparation. This lineup was pictured in front of our new "factory" in Venice, California. We acquired our new digs from Lance Reventlow, who had built his line of successful Scarab sports racing and disastrous Formula 1 cars there. Reventlow was forced to close down as the Internal Revenue Service declared he could only run his business in the red for so many years before paying taxes.

Right
Riverside Test, 1962
The first test day at Riverside for the new Cobra race car, chassis number CSX2002, with veteran driver Bill Krause at the wheel. The September 1962 test showed some of the racing modifications done to the car: Cooling slots were added on the tip of the nose; brake scoops were placed underneath the bumper overriders; a racing windscreen replaced the tall production windshield; and the required rollbar had been added. Bill Krause was impressed with the car's potential.

Shelby Goes Racing
Debut Duel With the Corvettes at Riverside

Our first race car made its debut at Riverside in October 1962 with Bill Krause driving. This race was a three-hour endurance that was run on Saturday, October 13, 1962, as a prelude to the famous *Los Angeles Times* Grand Prix for Sports Cars. This enduro was also the debut of the Corvette Z06, and the Chevrolet guys came loaded for bear with drivers like Dave MacDonald, Bob Bondurant, Jerry Grant, and Doug Hooper.

The endurance race was reasonably close at the beginning with Dave MacDonald's Corvette and Krause's Cobra swapping position for the lead in the early laps. Soon, however, the Cobra pulled away to a half-lap lead, only to have a wheel hub break and rob Shelby American of a victory in its premiere race.

Riverside Endurance Race, 1962
The Cobra's debut was spoiled by a broken hub carrier. The day after the race, Phil Remington was at work designing and building a new, stronger hub carrier. This problem never occurred again.

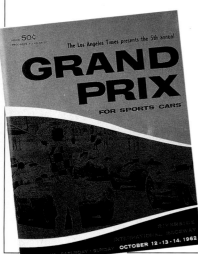

Riverside Endurance Race, 1962
At a little before 2pm on Saturday, October 13, 1962, Phil Remington drives the Cobra from the pit to the starting grid for its racing debut. Note the hood louvers for cooling that had been added after the testing session.

Left
Program for the 1962 *Los Angeles Times* Grand Prix at Riverside where Bill Krause drove the 260ci Cobra in its first race, the three-hour enduro scheduled before the actual Grand Prix.

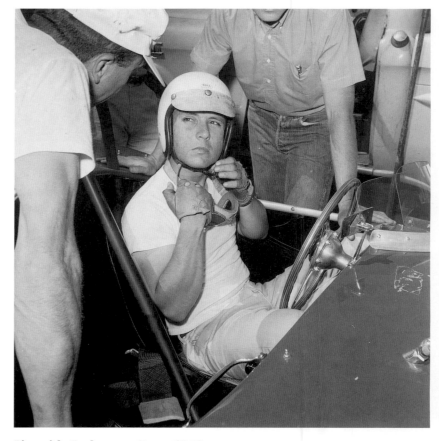

Riverside Endurance Race, 1962
Driver Bill Krause receives last-minute instructions from Carroll Shelby.

Riverside Endurance Race, 1962
After a bad start, Krause drifts the Cobra through Turn 6 in pursuit of Dave MacDonald's Corvette. The XP painted on the door stands for "Experimental Production," a class devised for this race only that allowed the Cobra and the Corvette Z06s to compete in the event. Krause took the lead from MacDonald on Lap 9 and pulled away to what seemed like a certain victory.

Bahamas Racing Vacation
Cobra vs. Ferrari at Nassau

In December 1962, the factory Cobra was sent to The Bahamas to compete in the Nassau Speed Weeks with Bill Krause driving. This event also saw the debut of the first two customer race cars, driven by privateer John Everly and Augie Pabst for Holman & Moody. Again, the Cobras were fast and impressive, but did not finish due to a number of teething problems.

Left
Nassau Speed Week, 1962
Bill Krause was impressive at Nassau. He ran well enough to give notice to the Ferrari 250 GTOs that the Cobra challenge would be serious. If it hadn't been for a slight miscalculation in refueling, the Cobra might have won its first race at Nassau.

Right
Nassau Speed Week, 1962
Bill Krause in Cobra #98 talks to his mechanic Don Pike while John Everly in #106 prepares for the race. Everly had the first customer race car.

Nassau Speed Week, 1962
The next race for the new Cobra was at Nassau in December 1962. Here, three Cobras are being off-loaded on the Nassau dock. Cobra #18 was a Holman & Moody entry to be driven by Augie Pabst in his sole race in a Cobra.

Shelby's Driving School
How to Drive—and Crash—Your Cobra

The Carroll Shelby School of High Performance Driving was created by Shelby American in 1962 to teach people high-performance driving. The classes took place at the nearby Riverside racetrack.

Revolutionary at the time, the Shelby school was the forerunner to the many high-performance driving schools in existence today.

Carroll Shelby School of High Performance Driving, 1962
Sometimes the unexpected happens. This was the reward for wrecking the school's Cobra. Fortunately this sort of thing rarely happened.

Carroll Shelby School of High Performance Driving, 1962
Carroll Shelby and Pete Brock demonstrate the fine art of achieving the proper line through a corner to two students at the Shelby driving school. Many hours were spent demonstrating technique on the blackboard before the students got into the cars. When the student successfully completed the prescribed course, they were given a plaque as a certificate of graduation.

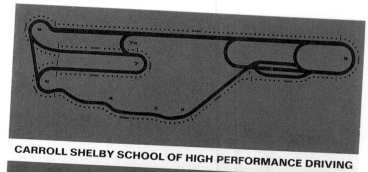

CARROLL SHELBY SCHOOL OF HIGH PERFORMANCE DRIVING

Brochure for the Carroll Shelby School of High Performance Driving.

Right
Carroll Shelby School of High Performance Driving, 1962
John Timanus (with blue Cobra team shirt) instructs one of the students at the Carroll Shelby School of High Performance Driving on how to properly drive a Cobra at Riverside. This Cobra was one of the school cars. Pete Brock (background) and Timanus were two of the best and most experienced instructors in the business. Their skill at communication with the student and understanding and solving their problems made the Shelby Driving School successful.

Endurance Race, Riverside, 1963
Dan Gurney pulls the Cobras of Allen Grant and Lew Spencer into Turn 7 at Riverside while leading the three-hour endurance race at Riverside in October 1963. Gurney led most of the race but had to stop and borrow a pocketknife from a spectator to fix an ignition problem near the end of the race. He finally finished fourth.

Chapter 2

1963

The Year Of Living Dangerously

The year 1963 brought incredible success to our small company. It seemed that we could do no wrong and victory was everywhere. It gave us a feeling of invincibility, and we believed that with the talent we had there was nothing we couldn't achieve.

Orders for production cars took off based on Carroll Shelby's uncanny promotional work in 1962. Every automobile magazine was knocking on Shelby America's door asking to test a car. At first, we only had the one car, CSX2000, which we repainted on almost a weekly basis to give the world the idea Shelby Cobras were pouring off our makeshift assembly line. In the early months of 1963, we had several cars available to show off.

By midyear, orders for production cars were coming in faster than we could build the new cars, so our Carter Street works were enlarged to handle the workload.

1963 Shelby American Championship poster celebrating the three championships won by Shelby American in its first year of racing. This poster is one of the rarest posters on the market today.

This also put a strain on AC Cars in England as our demand tested the small factory's production capabilities.

This was probably the pinnacle year for Shelby American with success on every front. As our poster of the time stated, Shelby American won three championships in 1963—our first year of taking on the world.

The year ended with our team traveling to The Bahamas for Nassau Speed Week. What a disaster! The team Cobras were buried by the hot-rod Corvette Grand Sports and our King Cobras were not competitive against the Chevy-powered Scarab of A. J. Foyt, Chaparrals of Jim Hall and Hap Sharp, and the Cooper-Chevy of Roger Penske.

It was a warning and a prelude to the coming year, 1964, which would bring some harsh realities to the forefront and many new lessons would be learned.

Fame Comes Calling
"Hey Little Cobra" Tops the Charts

As word of the performance of the street cars spread, Shelby American became a gathering place for the rich and famous as they all came to Venice to test drive the car. Among those who took demo rides and bought cars were Steve McQueen, Wilt Chamberlain, Bill Cosby, Jack Paar, Vic Damone, and James Garner.

Right
In late 1963, song writer Carol Connors wrote the popular Top 40 song "Hey Little Cobra." The song was inspired by her ownership of a Cobra and was recorded by The Rip Chords. Connors first become famous as the lead singer of The Teddy Bears when they recorded their huge late-fifties hit "To Know Him Is To Love Him."

Shelby American Factory, 1963
In June 1963, Steve McQueen paid a visit to Shelby American and a few days later took delivery of his 289 Cobra from Carroll Shelby in front of the Princeton Street race shop.

Right
The Rip Chords' "Hey Little Cobra and Other Hot Rod Hits" album became a Top 40 hit in 1963.

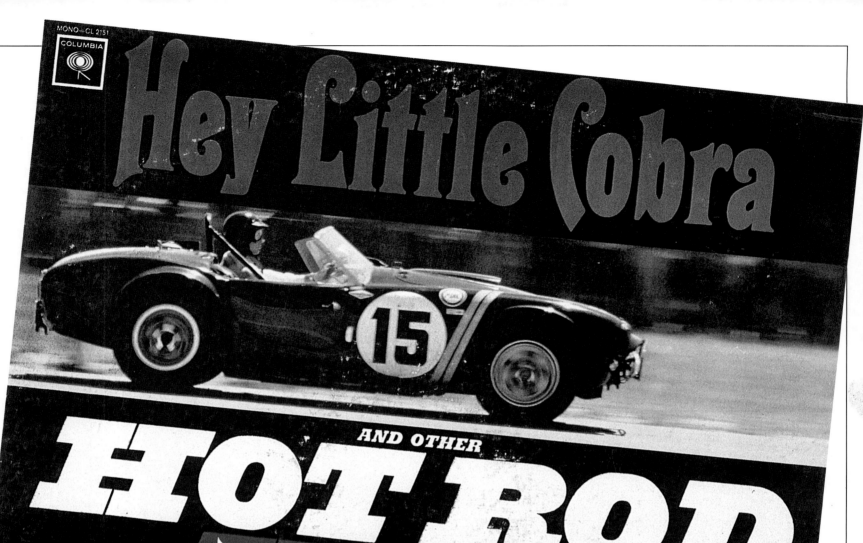

Hey Little Cobra

AND OTHER

HOT ROD HITS

THE RIP CHORDS

Hey Little Cobra / Here I Stand / The Queen / 409 / Ding Dong
'40 Ford Time / Gone / She Thinks I Still Care
Little Deuce Coupe / Trophy Machine / Shut Down / Drag City

GUARANTEED HIGH FIDELITY

Inside AC Cars
Building the Cobra Chassis

The AC Cars factory was working at capacity to complete Cobra chassis and bodies to be shipped to California. Our demand for cars was growing at a fast rate, and AC Cars was doing all it could to keep apace.

AC Cars Factory, 1963
Beginnings of a Cobra chassis. The large longitudinal tubes awaited the crossmembers and bridge structures at both end.

Right
AC Cars Factory, 1963
An AC Cars worker welds chassis tubes into place.

Left
AC Cars Factory, 1963
With tubes welded into place, the bare chassis was moved to the paint shop on a dolly, where the chassis was painted black. The chassis was then placed on another type of dolly that could be moved along the assembly line track as each task was completed.

On the AC Assembly Line
Hand-Building Production Cars

AC Cars Factory, 1963
With all of the interpanels attached to the subframe, the cars await the outer body. All of the chassis' and subframes were painted black.

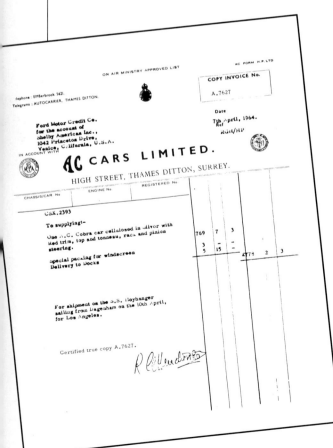

Left
Original invoice from AC Cars for supplying "One A.C. Cobra car cellulosed in silver with Red trim, top and tonneau, rack and pinion steering." This invoice was for CSX2393 and was dated April 7, 1964. Total cost of the car to Shelby American was £778/2/3, roughly equal to $1,500US. Note that the invoice was made out to "Ford Motor Credit Co. for the account of Shelby American Inc."
Tom Warth Collection

Right
AC Cars Factory, 1963
Cobra chassis on the assembly line with CSX2565 in the forefront. Brake components were the first items to be mounted, followed by the initial aluminum interpanels panels. Next, suspension, steering, and some electrics were added.

Clothing the Chassis
Finishing the Bodywork

AC Cars Factory, 1963
With the bare body installed on the chassis, the whole unit awaits a trip to the paint booth.

AC Cars Factory, 1963
The cars' bodywork was then painted at the AC paint facility. Cars here were being detailed out and readied for shipment to Shelby American. The cars were trucked to the London docks where they were loaded onto ship for the trip to Long Beach, California.

AC Cars Factory, 1963
After receiving a primer coat, the car was sanded out before the final paint is applied

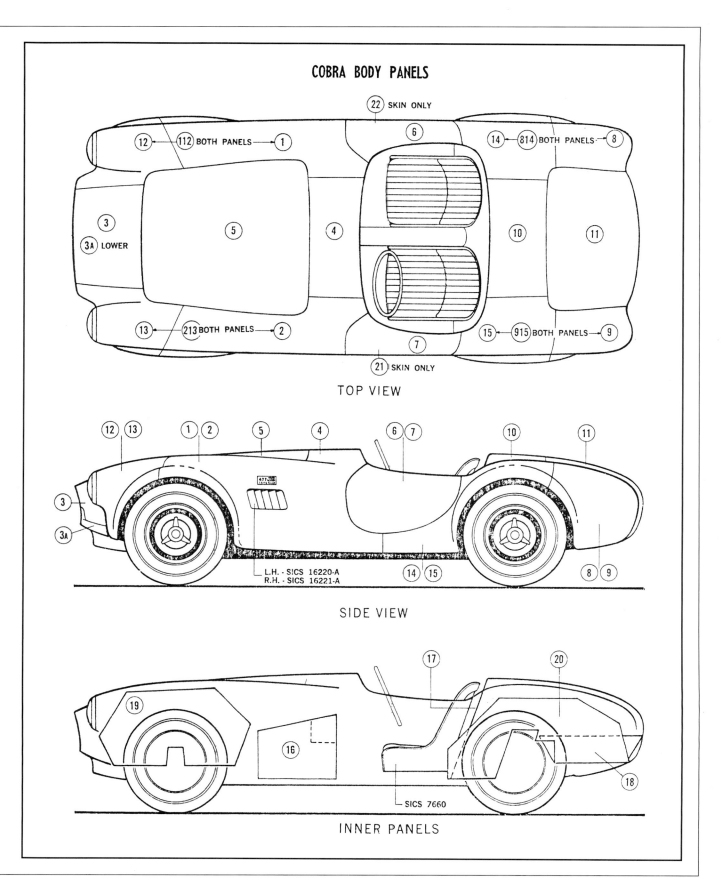

COBRA BODY PANELS

TOP VIEW

22 SKIN ONLY
12 ← 112 BOTH PANELS → 1
6
14 ← 814 BOTH PANELS → 8
3
3A LOWER
5
4
10
11
13 ← 213 BOTH PANELS → 2
7
15 ← 915 BOTH PANELS → 9
21 SKIN ONLY

SIDE VIEW

12 13   1 2   5   4   6 7   10   11
3
3A
477
L.H. - SICS 16220-A
R.H. - SICS 16221-A
14 15
8 9

INNER PANELS

17   20
19
16
SICS 7660
18

Right
Cobra Body Panels
Twenty-two panels went into one Cobra body, as shown in this parts book from 1968 that covered 1963–1967 Cobras. The drawing outlines a later 427 car. *Tom Warth Collection*

The Shoehorned Engine
On the Shelby American "Production Line"

By mid 1963, the production car orders were coming in faster then we could build the cars, and we enlarged our Carter Street facility to it's maximum capacity.

Each of the Cobras was hand built by a team of skilled mechanics who put a lot of themselves into the building of these cars. It was said by the men that built these cars that no two Cobras were the same, they all had their own individual personalities.

Shelby American Factory, 1963
A line of stock 289ci Ford V-8 engines the way they arrived at Shelby American from Ford. All of the 289 engines were stored on stands in a corner of the production facility. It was on these stands that the transmissions were installed along with some of the custom Cobra features.

Shelby American Factory, 1963
When the cars arrived at Shelby American, they were stored in a corner of the production facility on Carter Street to await final assembly.

Right
Shelby American Factory, 1963
Engine and transmission being lowered into a Cobra. The boxes in the cockpit contained the options to be installed as per customer order.

Shelby American Factory, 1963
The engine being bolted into place. The paper taped to the nose of the car was a check-off list detailing all of the work and options to be done to this particular car. When each task was completed, it was signed off by the mechanic's initials.

The Hot Rod Sports Car
Adding the Horsepower, Shelby Style

It was amazing that so many cars were built in the Carter Street facility. Everything was done in the same small building. Engines were stored in one corner, chassis stored in another, the paint booth was erected in another corner, and the parts department organized in the other. In between all of this were the ramps on which the cars were assembled and the engines installed.

To any outsider who saw this unique assembly line, it couldn't possibly work. But it did work—and it worked well.

Shelby American Factory, 1963
The Cobra 289 engine in its finished state.

Shelby American Factory, 1963
This car was being cleaned up after painting. Note that the Cobra badge has now been installed.

Right
Shelby American Factory, 1963
The custom Cobra valve covers being installed—note valve cover gasket waiting on the windshield. The nose of this car has been repaired due to the damage caused by the careless way that the cars were stored on the ships. Many cars required extensive body repairs, and I was constantly photographing damaged cars for the never ending insurance claims.

Left
Shelby American Factory, 1963
After repair bodywork and paint, the cars were returned to the "assembly line" where they received their tops, bumpers, and a final checkout before the road test.

Ready For Delivery
Cobra With Standard Equipment: $5,995

One of the best perks of being a Shelby American employee at that time was the loose policy that Shelby had about borrowing street cars from the sales department for the weekend. All that was ever required from us was a promise to bring the car back in one piece, and too my knowledge, no car was ever damaged by any of the employees.

I often took my friends from outside Shelby American for 130mph demonstration rides on the newly completed San Diego Freeway. I never scared them too badly and I never got caught by the Highway Patrol, although they tried several different times.

Going on a date in those cars drew maximum attention and my girlfriend Susan always enjoyed riding in those cars. Of course, I never demonstrated the car's full potential to her. There was never a shortage of valets wanting to park your car when you pulled into a restaurant parking lot, and I have never known such attention or prompt service since.

Right
The 1963 289ci Cobra price list with all of the option packages broken out.

Shelby American Factory, 1963
The car received a final cleaning and detailing prior to customer delivery.

42

Shelby American Factory, 1963
After the road test, final engine and brake adjustments were made.

Left
Shelby American Factory, 1963
The final product ready to take on all comers.

Cobra Victorious!
The Cobra's First Race Win

The new year saw the departure of Bill Krause as team driver and the signing of Ken Miles and Dave MacDonald as factory drivers.

The last race for the 260ci version of the Cobra was also the first race win for the marque. This victory came at Riverside on the weekend of February 2–3, 1963, with MacDonald taking the win both days over an impressive field of competitors. Ken Miles finished second both days giving Shelby American our first sweep of the top two spots, something that would be repeated many times in the next two and a half years.

Riverside SCCA race program from the Cobra's debut victory.

Riverside, 1963
Dave MacDonald scored the first Cobra win at Riverside in a SCCA race on February 2–3, 1963. MacDonald took the win on both days with Ken Miles in another Cobra finishing second. These were the only factory wins for the 260ci Cobras. The 289 was on the way.

Probably the most famous and recognized racing team jacket of all time. The 1963–1964 Shelby American Cobra team jacket is one of the most sought after collector's items in the world.

Cobras Against the World
Shelby American's First FIA Race

The first Fédération Internationale de l'Automobile race for Shelby was the Daytona Continental held on February 11, 1963. In spite of being down on top speed due to the lack of streamlining, the Cobras driven by Dan Gurney, Skip Hudson, and Dave MacDonald gave a good account of themselves against a strong field of Ferrari 250 GTOs, Corvettes, Porsches, and other assorted machinery.

Hudson actually led the race, swapping the lead with Pedro Rodriguez's winning GTO for a number of laps before crashing due to a blown flywheel that tried to cut off Hudson's foot. Dave MacDonald finished a creditable fourth behind a formidable trio of GTOs.

Daytona Continental, 1963
The Cobra team's first FIA race was at Daytona in February 1963. Skip Hudson performed brilliantly in his debut race in a Cobra. Early in the event, his hood came up and he had to stop and shut it. He eventually caught up to race leader Pedro Rodriguez's Ferrari and was involved in an intense battle for the lead when the Cobra's flywheel exploded, breaking Hudson's foot and putting him in the hospital. Note the hood coming ajar in this photo. Dave MacDonald drove the only Cobra (#99) to finish the Daytona race, coming in fourth.

Daytona Continental, 1963
Dan Gurney's first race in a Cobra was a typical Gurney race. A last-minute engine change put Gurney on the track with two laps gone. Gurney charged through the field and was up to fifth when problems sidelined him on Lap 48.

First Win for the 289
Dave MacDonald Takes the Checkered Flag

The premiere race for the 289ci Cobra was at Dodger Stadium in Los Angeles on the weekend of March 2–3, 1963. Dave MacDonald again won both days with Ken Miles finishing second.

Dodger Stadium, Los Angeles, 1963
Dave and Sherry MacDonald take a victory lap at the Dodger Stadium races in February 1963. Sherry MacDonald remembers the Shelby years: " I didn't go to as many races as I would have liked because our kids were too young. I did go to most of the races on the West Coast and I went to Nassau in 1963. I used to get so mad at Carroll because he wouldn't let Dave win all of the races. When you are young and married to a guy who you think is the best and the fastest, you want him to win them all."

Shelby Attacks Sebring
Testing the Cobra's Mettle Over 12 Hours

At Sebring in March 1963, the Cobras suffered from every possible malfunction known to man. Only one car of the entry of six managed to finish: Phil Hill, Lew Spencer, and Ken Miles brought their trouble-plagued Cobra home in a creditable eleventh place overall.

Left
Sebring Press Conference, 1963
Carroll Shelby, far left, announced his team for Sebring at a press conference in early March 1963. The team would include, from left, Dan Gurney, Phil Hill, Peter Jopp, Lew Spencer, Dave MacDonald, and Ken Miles.

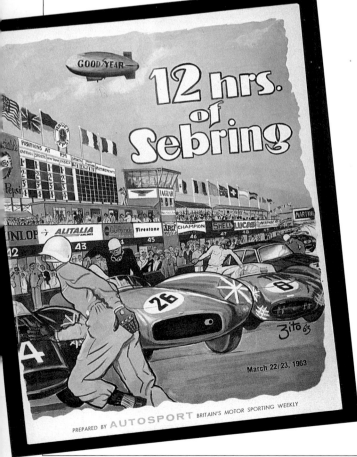

Right
12 Hours of Sebring, 1963
Dan Gurney races through Sebring's famous Webster Turn. Last-minute race preparations meant that Gurney's Cobra was "painted with a spray can," as Pete Brock remembered.

Left
1963 Sebring race program.

12 Hours of Sebring
An Onslaught of Mechanical Woes

12 Hours of Sebring, 1963
Ken Miles, at the wheel of the car that he originally shared with Lew Spencer at Sebring in 1963. Miles leads the Ferrari 250 GTO of Charlie Hayes and Doug Thiem.

12 Hours of Sebring, 1963
Ken Miles at speed during the 1963 Sebring race. Shelby remembered Miles as "contributing more to our racing program then anyone can ever imagine. He did everything for us, and he did it well."

12 Hours of Sebring, 1963
Phil Hill made a spectacular start in this Cobra and led the first couple laps of the 1963 Sebring race. This was the only Cobra to finish in a decent position. The car finished eleventh overall and eighth in GT, but it did finish first in the GT 14/15 category.

12 Hours of Sebring, 1963
Dave MacDonald in the Cobra that he shared with stock-car legend Glenn "Fireball" Roberts at Sebring in March 1963. This car DNFed due to rear-end problems.

12 Hours of Sebring
Battling the Ferrari GTO

12 Hours of Sebring, 1963
The great stock car driver Fireball Roberts in his only ride in a Cobra. Roberts co-drove with Dave MacDonald at the 1963 Sebring race, but the car left the race early with rear end trouble.

Right
12 Hours of Sebring, 1963
Dan Gurney accelerates away from the hairpin during the 1963 Sebring race. Dan Gurney challenged Roger Penske's Ferrari 250 GTO for the GT class lead with this Cobra until gremlins set in. Gurney remembers the Cobra as "being a driver friendly car. You could take it to the limits and then some without getting into trouble."

12 Hours of Sebring, 1963
Late afternoon at Sebring in March 1963 and the Dan Gurney/Phil Hill Cobra limps on to a twenty-ninth-place finish. As with all of the Cobras that year, this car suffered its share of mechanical problems.

12 Hours of Sebring, 1963
Dan Gurney takes a brief driving stint in the Cobra originally co-driven by Lew Spencer and Ken Miles. The Cobra team had so many mechanical problems at Sebring in 1963 that the drivers hopped from one car to another depending on which cars were running at the time. Gurney passes the Corvette driven by Jerry Grant and Don Campbell.

Right
12 Hours of Sebring, 1963
Ken Miles is checking for gremlins at the side of the track. He found plenty with this car's steering, which eventually put him out of the race.

War of the USRRC
Cobras Sweep the Tracks Clean

As the season progressed, the Cobras began dominating all of the United States Road Racing Championship (USRRC) and Sports Car Club of America (SCCA) events.

Famed East Coast driver Bob Holbert joined the team in late March and became the first driver to win the inaugural USRRC driver's championship. Shelby American also won the USRRC manufacturer's championship, Bob Johnson won the SCCA A-Production championship, and Dan Gurney won the first FIA race for Shelby American by taking the checkered flag at the Bridgehampton 500 on September 14, 1963.

Del Mar, 1963
Dave MacDonald tried desperately to catch Bill Sherwood's Corvette Z06 at Del Mar in April 1963. MacDonald spun out and lost the race. This was the only defeat to the Shelby team by a Corvette during our racing years.

Right
Continental Divide USRRC, 1963
After years of driving those Corvettes, Bob Bondurant made his debut in a Cobra and Dave MacDonald drove the only Le Mans hardtop (#97) to race in this country, at the USRRC race at Continental Divide in August 1963. Bondurant finished fifth overall but won the GT race. MacDonald finished second.

Left
1963 Watkins Glen USRRC race won by the Cobra of Bob Johnson

War of the USRRC
Cobra vs. Corvette

1963 USRRC race at Laguna Seca won by Bob Holbert's Cobra.

Laguna Seca USRRC, 1963
Bob Holbert leads Ken Miles on his way to winning the USRRC race at Laguna Seca in June 1963.

Road America June Sprints, 1963
Two of the East Coast's most famous rivals go at it during the Road America June Sprints in 1963. Bob Johnson in his Cobra and Dick Thompson in the Grady Davis Corvette were good friends and fierce rivals during this era. Johnson won this race with Thompson finishing third.

Cobras at Le Mans
The Snake's First Strike

The Cobra's first appearance at the 24 Hours of Le Mans came in June 1963. Two teams entered Cobras for Le Mans, each with one car. American Cobra dealer Ed Hugus co-drove with Peter Jopp but the team was a DNF.

AC Cars campaigned the other entry, which was driven by Peter Harper and Ninian Sanderson. The AC Cobra finished sixth overall.

Both Cobras ran fitted with the "Le Mans" hardtops, the first effort to improve the car's less-than-perfect aerodynamics.

24 Hours of Le Mans, 1963
American Cobra dealer Ed Hugus at the wheel of his Cobra entry. Co-driving with Peter Jopp, the Cobra ran well but did not finish.

Road America 500
Miles and Holbert Rule the Race

Road America 500, 1963
Ken Miles prepares for the start of the 1963 Road America 500. Miles and co-driver Bob Holbert finished a strong second overall in that race Mechanics (in red team shirts) Louie Unser, by the right front fender, and Red Pierce assisted Miles with the seatbelt.

Road America 500, 1963
A pit stop at the 1963 Road America 500 for the Ken Miles/Bob Holbert Cobra. Miles is at the rear of the car in the dark green helmet while Bob Holbert (in white helmet at the far left) prepares to enter the car after refueling. Mechanics Jim Culleton, changing the left front brake pads. and Red Pierce, holding the fuel hose, work a well-coordinated pit stop.

Road America 500, 1963
By September 1963, this team truck and trailer became one of the most recognized and feared sights in American road racing.

Road America 500
A Ride to Victory Lane

Road America 500, 1963
Lew Spencer arrived at his pit minus his left front wheel and, with the help of Carroll Shelby, jacked the car up so that the mechanics could repair the damage and replace the wheel.

Right
Road America 500, 1963
Bob Holbert and Ken Miles in victory lane at the Road America 500 in September 1963.

Bridgehampton 500
The Cobra's First FIA Victory

1963 Bridgehampton 500 program.

Below
Bridgehampton 500, 1963
Dan Gurney drives the Cobra to its first FIA win at the Bridgehampton 500 on September 14, 1963. Two years later, the Cobra team would make its final appearance and win its final FIA race at this event.

Canadian Grand Prix
Ken Miles Motors to a Win

**Canadian Grand Prix,
Mosport, 1963**
Trophy won by Ken Miles in the GT class
of the Canadian Grand Prix at Mosport in
September 1963.

Right
**Canadian Grand Prix,
Mosport, 1963**
Ken Miles driving the Comstock Racing
Team Cobra on his way to victory in the
GT class race at the Canadian Grand Prix
at Mosport in September 1963.

Left
Ken Miles sips a Pepsi and signs
autographs for admiring youngsters
at Mosport.

Santa Barbara Road Races
Allen Grant's Big Ride

Santa Barbara Road Races, 1963
Ole Olsen and Allen Grant pose with their beautiful race car and tow truck prior to the car's initial outing at Santa Barbara in September 1963. This photograph was taken next to the Shelby American Carter Street production building in Venice, California. Allen's long-time friend George Lucas designed the paint scheme and the car turned out to be, in my opinion, the most beautiful Cobra race car of the whole bunch. Lucas went on to fame producing and directing many popular films.

Right
Santa Barbara Road Races, 1963
Allen Grant behind the wheel of the beautiful Coventry Motors Cobra. Grant and his Cobra led the arch-rival Chevrolet Corvettes of Doug Hooper, Paul Reinhart, and Scott Briley at the twentieth running of the famed Santa Barbara Road Races, in September 1963. Grant remembered: "This was my first big ride and I wanted to impress Shelby so that I could get a factory ride in 1964. I didn't want to screw up and I was scared to death at the start of the race. I had some of the best competition of the year in that race; all of the best Corvette guys from the West Coast were there. I was facing well-known veterans like Bob Bondurant, Bill Krause, Paul Reinhart, Dick Guldstrand, and Doug Hooper—and these guys were all out to beat me. I got good starts both days and managed to pull away from the Corvettes and win both days. It was a thrill to win my first two races in that car."

Building the King Cobra
The Cooper With Fangs

By mid-summer, Shelby American received our first Cooper Monaco chassis and we began modifying it so it would accept our 289ci Ford V-8 engine. Dave MacDonald, Wally Peat, and Ole Olsen did most of the original work on the project, and the results were sensational from the start. The initial test at Riverside with Dave MacDonald at the wheel resulted in numerous laps turned under the official record.

Shelby American crew chief and mechanic Wally Peat remembered when the first of the Cooper chassis arrived in August 1963: "When the Cooper chassis arrived from England, the first thing I had to do was re-weld the chassis tubes. The chassis tubes were the weak point of those cars, and I was always having to re-weld the frames at the races. Those frames were just not made for the types of speeds that we were running or the stress we were putting on them. They were made to be run with a four-cylinder Climax engine, not a Ford or a Chevy V-8. The cars handled good, just so long as the cracks in the frame didn't open up too much.

"We also had to change quite a bit of the cooling system and we had to adapt the frame to accommodate the Ford engine and Colotti gearbox. We cut the windshields down and changed the location of the radiators. We also had to make quite a bit of special linkage for the engine and transmission, and we had to build the exhaust systems."

The so-called King Cobra first raced at Kent, Washington, in September 1963, with both Bob Holbert and MacDonald setting new lap records. Unfortunately overheating problems kept either of them from finishing or from victory.

Shelby American Factory, 1963
Dave MacDonald sits in the first Cooper Monaco chassis to arrive at Shelby American in mid-August 1963. Carroll Shelby looks on with approval.

Shelby American Factory, 1963
Another view of the near-complete King Cobra. Note that the drag race-style exhaust pipes have now been installed.

Left
Riverside, 1963
Dave MacDonald tests the King Cobra at Riverside in September 1963. MacDonald was well under the lap record during this test. Wally Peat remembered: "The big advantage that I had with Dave was that he worked at the shop and we could always test new ideas for his car. Bob Holbert lived in Pennsylvania and he didn't come out except for the races. That made it difficult to change things on his car. We had the radiator on Dave's car tilted forward and he didn't have the cooling problems that Holbert had with his car. Holbert's radiator stood straight up in the chassis."

Kent FIA Race, 1963

Dave MacDonald prepares to enter his car prior to the first race for the King Cobra, at Kent, Washington, in September 1963. Crew chief Wally Peat is seen on the left and Craig Lang is behind MacDonald. MacDonald's car retired due to overheating, but not before leading the race and setting a lap record. The potential of the King Cobra was proven.

Left
Shelby American Factory, 1963

Dave MacDonald and Ole Olsen install the engine in the Cooper chassis in August 1963.

Riverside Endurance Race
Allen Grant, "Constipated Bull"

In the three-hour endurance race prior to the *Los Angeles Times* Grand Prix at Riverside in October 1963, there was a fearsome battle for the victory between a snakepit of Cobras. Allen Grant remembered: "I was really primed for this race, it was my first big opportunity to race against the factory team. Shelby had Gurney, Bondurant, and Spencer in the race and I had warned him that I would blow them all off. My mechanic, Ole Olsen, had built a very strong engine for this race, but I didn't qualify as well as I should have. I was fifth on the grid behind the three factory cars and Ginther's Ferrari GTO. To make matters worse, we had to replace a water hose that broke on the starting grid.

"I got a great start and was second going into Turn 6 when Bondurant rear ended me and I spun out in the middle of the turn. I was really mad and when I re-joined the race in tenth place, I could hardly control myself. By lap four, I was back up to fourth place and gaining on the factory cars. By the end of the race I was back up to second and gaining on Bondurant, who won the race. If the race had gone one lap further, I would have won because Bondurant blew a tire in Turn 1 on the cool off lap.

"Somebody wrote in one of the magazines that 'I charged through the field like a constipated bull.' That was a name I was never able to live down throughout the rest of my days at Shelby American."

Endurance Race, Riverside, 1963
On the first lap, Gurney leads Grant (#96) and Bondurant (#99) into Turn 6. Bondurant is taking an inside line and Grant the normal outside line.

Endurance Race, Riverside, 1963
Bondurant taps Grant on the rear of his car forcing him to spin.

Left
Endurance Race, Riverside, 1963
Grant's competition on the starting grid. The Shelby American team on the front row consists of Bondurant (#99), Gurney (#97), and Spencer (#98).

Endurance Race, Riverside, 1963
A furious Allen Grant, leading factory Cobra driver Lew Spencer, charges into
Turn 7 at Riverside during a three-hour endurance race prior to the *Los Angeles
Times* Grand Prix in October 1963.

Los Angeles Times GP
The King Cobra Bites

After its disastrous debut, the tide turned for the King Cobra. Dave MacDonald scored a first ever sweep of the two biggest sports car races in the world, the *Los Angeles Times* Grand Prix at Riverside and the Pacific Grand Prix at Laguna Seca.

Bob Holbert suffered from overheating at Riverside, but set a lap record at Laguna Seca and led the race for many laps before retiring after colliding with a back marker while lapping the car.

The 1963 Times Grand Prix at Riverside and the Pacific Grand Prix at Laguna Seca—both won by Dave MacDonald in a King Cobra.

Right
***Los Angeles Times* Grand Prix, Riverside, 1963**
The Shelby American pit during the 1963 *Los Angeles Times* Grand Prix at Riverside. The factory entries of three Cobra roadsters and two King Cobras are plainly visible as Carroll Shelby (in black cowboy hat behind King Cobra #99) supervises preparation.

Los Angeles Times GP

"Passing Cars Like They Were Stopped"

Shelby American crew chief Wally Peat recalled Dave MacDonald's great victory at Riverside: "At the *Times* race, Dave was really dialed in—he was passing those guys like they were stopped. We started on the front row and we knew we could win if the car lasted the race. Our only worry was Jim Hall in his new Chaparral and our teammate Bob Holbert in the other King Cobra. When these two were eliminated in the early going, it made things a little easier.

"Dave lapped the entire international field that day, a feat that had never been done before in that race. Everyone who was there saw something very special that day; Dave and that car were absolutely unbeatable."

Right
Los Angeles Times Grand Prix, Riverside, 1963
Bob Bondurant had quite a weekend during the 1963 *Times* Grand Prix. He won the three-hour endurance race and came back in the Grand Prix to finish eighth overall against an international field of sports racing cars.

Below
Los Angeles Times Grand Prix, Riverside, 1963
Dave MacDonald leads Bob Holbert out of Turn 6 at the *Times* Grand Prix at Riverside in October 1963. This photo became the most widely distributed King Cobra photos of them all and also one of the most-famous.

Los Angeles Times GP
The Flying Dave McDonald

***Los Angeles Times* Grand Prix, Riverside, 1963**
A jubilant Carroll Shelby gives pit signals to the flying MacDonald.

Los Angeles Times Grand Prix, Riverside, 1963
Craig Lang pushes the Dave MacDonald King Cobra back from the Riverside pits as Ken Miles steers.

Los Angeles Times GP
MacDonald Laps the International Field

Chaparral creator Jim Hall remembered the *Times* Grand Prix race against Dave MacDonald, "The Master of Oversteer": "The first time I followed Dave through Turn 6 at Riverside, he scared the hell out of me. After a couple of laps I figured out that was just the way he drove. Dave was the only driver that could challenge the Chaparrals during the first part of the 1964 season. His death at Indianapolis was a real loss."

Los Angeles Times Grand Prix, Riverside, 1963
An exhausted Dave MacDonald gets a quick bath prior to receiving his rewards of victory at Riverside. MacDonald had lapped the international field in 90 degree plus heat.

Right
Los Angeles Times Grand Prix, Riverside, 1963
Dave MacDonald, "the Master of Oversteer," powers his King Cobra out of Turn 6 at Riverside during the 1963 *Times* Grand Prix. MacDonald lapped an international field during the 1963 race, the first driver to ever do so in this race.

Pacific Grand Prix
MacDonald Repeats Himself

Pacific Grand Prix, Laguna Seca, 1963
Dave MacDonald leads Jim Hall's new rear-engined Chaparral 2 out of Laguna Seca's Turn 9 during the 1963 Pacific Grand Prix.

Dave MacDonald repeated his ride to Victory Line by winning the Pacific Grand Prix at Laguna Seca one week after the Riverside win. But at Laguna, it was a totally different story. Crew chief Wally Peat remembered: "During qualifying on Friday we blew our engine, and Dave had to settle for thirteenth qualifying position. We replaced the engine, but in the warm-ups on Sunday morning, Dave crashed. He went off the track at Turn 2 and bent the frame. We had to try and straighten the frame by race time and we used the trailer ramps to try and line that car up. We got the car to the grid just in time for the start.

"When the green flag dropped he fell back to eighteenth position because the transmission was jumping out of gear. As the race progressed, Dave started his move and by Lap 52, he took the lead. He had to work hard for every position since this field was just about the same as we saw at Riverside. We were really sweating out the finish and when Dave took the win, all hell broke loose.

"We partied all night on the champagne that all of the crew had stolen from the big party after the race. Everyone had long coats on at that party because it was so cold up there at night. We all loaded up our pockets with bottles and everyone was clanking when they left that party and headed for our motel. I remember that everyone was so drunk that we lined up on the balcony and started throwing champagne glasses into the swimming pool to see if we could get them to stand up straight on the bottom of the pool. People were jumping off the balcony into the pool and there was a craps game going on in one of the rooms.

"The next morning, Carroll Shelby came into my room and said, 'Wally, you and your gangsters get out there and clean up that damn mess.' From then on, all of us were known as 'Wally's Gangsters.'

"Those were the two races that Dave remembered the most. We won many other races, but it was nothing like what we did there. All of us had some wonderful times together, they were really special. The thing I liked best about those days was that we were all friends. Hall, Penske—it didn't matter, we all helped each other and cared about each other. Hall and Dave were bitter rivals on the track and they had some fabulous races. Off the track, however, they were the best of friends."

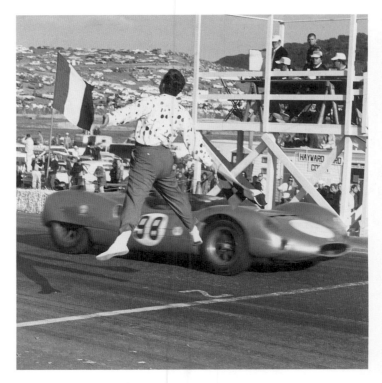

Pacific Grand Prix, Laguna Seca, 1963
MacDonald takes the checkered flag at Laguna Seca after coming from seventeenth place to defeat an international field.

Right

Pacific Grand Prix, Laguna Seca, 1963

MacDonald accepts the trophy and the check for his second major international win in two weeks. The parties celebrating the MacDonald victory were in full swing.

Below

Pacific Grand Prix, Laguna Seca, 1963

Two of Dave MacDonald's biggest win trophies. On the left, Pacific Grand Prix 1963 and on the right, Sebring 1964. Dave's Cobra helmet was one of the most famous, colorful, and recognizable of that period. He wore it in all of his most famous victories for Shelby American.

Chapter 3

1964

Sitting On Top Of The World

By January 1964, the Cobra coupe project was being rushed to completion and plans were being made for its race debut at Daytona on February 16. The coupe project was one of those impossible projects that no one outside our company could conceive us finishing on time.

At this time, our race shop was bursting at the seams. We were preparing Cobra roadsters, King Cobras, a prototype Sunbeam Tiger, a prototype 427 Cobra, customer race cars, and the Cobra coupe and two other coupe chassis—all in one small shop on Princeton Drive. How did we do it? Dedication—backed by long hours, no weekends off, no

This 289 Cobra was backed by an automatic transmission, although there was no outward appearance change. Approximately thirty 289 Cobras were built with automatic transmissions.

Left
Official Shelby American Sales Department photographs for a sale portfolio that was made for each person in the department to show to serious buyers. All of the different colors were pictured as well as most of the options.

holidays, little sleep, and precious little social life made it all happen and on time.

This was the year for Shelby American to invade Europe. We had swept the American championships in 1963; now we had to prove ourselves on the international circuit. Unfortunately, winning the FIA championship in our premiere year would be an unfulfilled dream, but we did give Ferrari notice that we were serious about taking away its crown. There was always 1965.

By the end of 1964, it was apparent that we had outgrown the Princeton and Carter Street facilities and larger quarters were needed. These facilities were found on Imperial Highway at the Los Angeles Airport, and the rest of 1964 was spent preparing to make the move in the Spring of 1965.

Cobra Sales Portfolio
The Shelby American Sales Photographs

I took these photographs for the Shelby American Sales Department in early 1964, and a set of prints was made for each person in that department to show to serious buyers. These photographs showed potential customers the different colors available and how the cars looked when they were finished. We also made sure that all of the styles of the finished car were shown in the sales album, including Cobras with and without the softtop and the hardtop option.

A 289 Cobra photographed with the optional hardtop, which was never a popular option.

Cobra Racers Portfolio
The Racing Department Sales Photographs

After seeing the photo book that the Sales Department and I created in order to sell production cars, the Racing Department thought it would be a good idea to do a book of their own. As with the sales book, the race book pictured various customer cars and showed potential clients what their options were.

A rare Shelby American Cobra team lightweight windbreaker, one of a very few that exist today.

Cobra Racers Portfolio
The Racing Department Sales Photographs

Building the Cobra Coupe
Pete Brock's Aerodynamic Masterpiece

One of the most challenging projects ever at Shelby American was the creation of the Cobra coupe, begun in October 1963. The Cobra coupe project became a reality during that time and work proceeded at top speed in order to have a car completed by the Daytona race the following February. The project was completed on time and the performance of the car was well beyond anyone's expectation.

Few people still believe that the coupe was completed and running in less then ninety days. Take it from one who photographed it on a daily basis: it did happen. I'm not sure that such a project, even with today's computer-aided design technology, could go from dream to completion in the time that we had allotted.

Shelby American Factory, 1963
Pete Brock and two helpers push the completed buck into position for loading onto a trailer for the trip to Cal Metal Shaping.

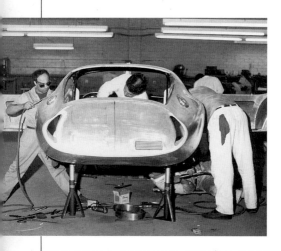

Right
Shelby American Factory, 1963
The first step was to build a buck for the bodywork. Ken Miles sits in the frame of the Cobra that was wrecked at Daytona while Dave MacDonald (in suit) and Pete Brock measure his desired headroom.

Left
Shelby American Factory, 1964
As 1964 began, the Cobra coupe neared completion. The rush was on to make Daytona, which was less than a month away. Fabricators were completing the body and getting the car ready to be wired.

Daytona Continental
Debut of the Cobra "Daytona" Coupe

Our first competition event for 1964 was the Daytona Continental 2,000km (1,243 miles) race on February 16. The Cobra coupe made a sensational debut with Dave MacDonald and Bob Holbert driving. The coupe lead the race and set numerous records until a freak pit fire robbed us of sure victory.

Dan Gurney and Bob Johnson drove a Cobra roadster on seven cylinders to finish fourth behind three Ferrari 250 GTOs.

Right
1964 Daytona Continental where the Cobra coupe made its spectacular debut.

Daytona Continental, 1964
The Daytona Continental in February 1964 was a spectacular debut for the Cobra coupe. Dave MacDonald and Bob Holbert lead a great many laps and were miles ahead when a freak pit fire sidelined the car

Right
Daytona Continental, 1964
Bob Johnson, who was co-driving with Dan Gurney, leads a Corvette and the Ferrari 250 GTO of Perkins/Eve through the first turn. This was the only Shelby entry to finish and it finished fourth, running on seven cylinders.

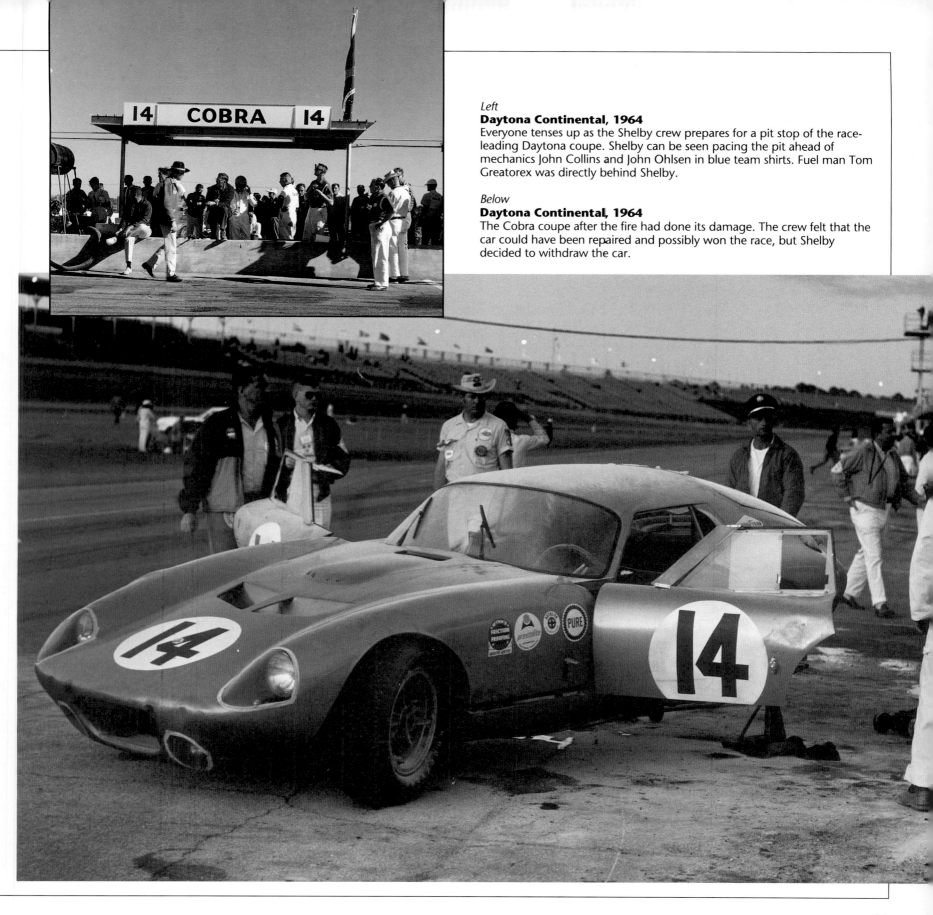

Left

Daytona Continental, 1964

Everyone tenses up as the Shelby crew prepares for a pit stop of the race-leading Daytona coupe. Shelby can be seen pacing the pit ahead of mechanics John Collins and John Ohlsen in blue team shirts. Fuel man Tom Greatorex was directly behind Shelby.

Below

Daytona Continental, 1964

The Cobra coupe after the fire had done its damage. The crew felt that the car could have been repaired and possibly won the race, but Shelby decided to withdraw the car.

Building the 427 Prototype
Ken Miles' Handiwork

The Shelby Cobra started off as an American hot rod version of a British sports car; we simply added 260ci worth of American V-8 power to an AC. This attitude naturally persisted throughout Shelby American's history and we were always in search of more horsepower.

Thus it should come as no surprise that when we happened to have a 427ci NASCAR engine sitting around the shop, someone would pull out the engine hoist and see if it would fit into a Cobra. With a little massaging, it was a perfect fit.

And so was born Ken Miles' new 427ci racer, the forerunner of the 427ci production Cobra.

Shelby American Factory, 1963
A 427ci NASCAR engine was spotted sitting on a pallet in the corner of the Shelby American race shop in December 1963. During a bench racing session one evening, someone asked, "What would happen if we put that thing into one of the Cobra chassis?"

Riverside, 1964
The 427 prototype was taken to Riverside for a test the same day that the coupe was first tested. Bob Bondurant was behind the steering wheel of the 427 for the test sessions: "I must have been nuts to drive that thing at racing speed with those wire wheels on. With that much power I could have easily pulled the spokes out of the wheels."

Shelby American Factory, 1963
Ken Miles listened and soon the engine was lowered into a 289 chassis after some "slight" modifications. Here, Ted Sutton works on the car as Ken Miles and Pete Brock discuss the progress of the Cobra coupe in the background.

Left
12 Hours of Sebring, 1964
When the 427 prototype arrived at Sebring, Ken Miles promptly hit a tree in practice causing major damage. Miles (left) and co-driver John Morton work into the night to repair the car. Al Dowd looks on in doubt.

12 Hours of Sebring
The Cobra Coupe's Premiere Win

We were back in force for the 12 Hours of Sebring with a full team of Cobra roadsters and coupes. The Cobra coupe proved its potential and took its first GT class win over the legion of Ferrari 250 GTOs on March 21, 1964.

12 Hours of Sebring, 1964
John Morton at the wheel of the prototype Cobra 427, which he shared with Ken Miles. Morton, a young Shelby American employee and successful West Coast club racer, got his chance to drive when Phil Hill opted for a ride in the 289 roadster with Jo Schlesser.

Right
12 Hours of Sebring, 1964
The Cobra Daytona coupe with Bob Holbert driving heads for its first GT win at Sebring in March 1964.

Inset
12 Hours of Sebring, 1964
Ken Miles at the wheel of the original Cobra 427 prototype at Sebring in 1964. Miles and co-driver John Morton kept this monster running until the engine finally blew late in the race. The car also suffered serious brake problems but showed potential for the future. Listening to this car go down the Warehouse Straight was a ground-shaking experience.

Left
1964 12 Hours of Sebring where the MacDonald/ Holbert Cobra coupe won its first race.

12 Hours of Sebring
Racing Through the Night

12 Hours of Sebring, 1964
Crew chief Charlie Agapiou signals Dave MacDonald where to stop as the Cobra coupe makes its final stop before finishing fourth overall and first in GT during the 1964 Sebring race. Mechanic Jim Culleton can be seen at the far right ready to assist.

12 Hours of Sebring, 1964
The fabulous Ferrari 250 GTO was the Cobra's chief rival throughout the early years of Shelby American's racing career. By 1964, the GTO was no match for the Cobra in speed, but in endurance racing it was still very much a threat. This GTO was driven by Ed Cantrell, Harry Heuer, and Don Yenko to twenty-eighth place.

Right
12 Hours of Sebring, 1964
The Shaw/Lund/Hayes Cobra #17 leads the Bondurant/Spencer Cobra #12 out of the Sebring Hairpin in 1964. A 1964 Ferrari GTO chases the two Cobras. The #17 Cobra went out of the race with brake failure after sixty-two laps while the Bondurant/Spencer Cobra went on to finish the race fifth overall.

12 Hours of Sebring, 1964
The fast Bob Johnson/Dan Gurney Cobra roadster led the GT class at Sebring in 1964 until a spectacular, fiery crash totally destroyed the car. It is interesting to note that this car has turned up at vintage races on the West Coast when, in fact, it was so badly damaged by the Sebring crash that it was cut up and thrown in the dumpster. The frame was actually broken in three places when what was left of the body was finally removed at the Shelby shop. Johnson recalled: "I don't remember anything about the crash, but when I saw what was left of the car the next day, I knew I was damn lucky to be alive."

12 Hours of Sebring
How to Turn a Cobra Into Scrap Metal

Left
12 Hours of Sebring, 1964
Because of his height, Dan Gurney felt more comfortable jumping over the door of the Cobra during a Le Mans start then entering through it.

Right
12 Hours of Sebring, 1964
Dan Gurney prepares to return to the 1964 Sebring race as Charlie Agapiou finishes wiping the windshield. Other crewman in blue team shirts on wall were Tony Stoer, Gary Kioke, Dave Peat, Jack Hoare, and Al Dowd (holding the fuel hose). Jim Culleton can be seen in the background behind Gurney.

12 Hours of Sebring, 1964
Gurney and co-driver Bob Johnson led the GT category and were running as high as fourth overall. Johnson took over the car and in the middle of the eleventh hour disaster struck. As Johnson passed the pits at over 125mph, he rear-ended an Alfa Romeo that was running without any lights. The Alfa exploded and Johnson's Cobra went end over end for several hundred feet, totally destroying the car. Carroll Shelby and Ken Miles feared for the worst; no one who saw the accident thought that either driver could have possibly survived. They both did, however, and Johnson had a black eye and a broken nose to show for his unwanted experience.

12 Hours of Sebring, 1964
What's left of the car sits on the floor of the Shelby Race Shop prior to being totally cut up and thrown in the dumpster. The frame was broken in at least three places and the tops of the Weber carburetors were completely ground down from sliding upside down.

12 Hours of Sebring
Cobras Sweep Away the Ferraris

12 Hours of Sebring, 1964
The Cobra of Phil Hill and Jo Schlesser rounds the Sebring Hairpin at sunset.

This car finished sixth overall and third in the GT class behind two other Cobras.

12 Hours of Sebring, 1964
The Ed Hugus entry of Ed Lowther and George Wintersteen had their share of problems during the race and finished thirty-fifth overall.

Left
1964 Shelby American Sebring victory poster.

Right
12 Hours of Sebring, 1964
In the last night pit stop before the finish, Lew Spencer straps himself into the Cobra he shared with Bob Bondurant during the 1964 Sebring race. This car finished fifth overall and second in the GT category.

Shelby Invades Europe
Battling Ferrari For the World Championship

After our victory at Sebring on March 21, Carroll Shelby called a press conference on Wednesday March 25, at the Ambassador Hotel in Los Angeles. Shelby announced that the Shelby American team would challenge the might of Europe for the FIA World Manufacturer's Championship.

For the next several months, we faced the immense task of running two race teams, one in Europe and the other on the US homefront. We also had commitments to other projects—including the Sunbeam Tiger, 427 Cobra, King Cobra, and GT350 Shelby Mustang—as well as customer cars to build and maintain. It seemed insurmountable, but we did it.

Within a week of the GT win at Sebring, Shelby called a press conference to tell the world that he planned to send a team to Europe to challenge Ferrari for the world championship.

The famous Cobra Team Shirt worn by the team in 1964 and 1965.

Targa Florio, April 1964

The first European race for the Cobra team was the Targa Florio in Sicily in April 1964. This was a race that the Cobras were definitely not designed to run. Jerry Grant and Dan Gurney were the only Cobra finishers, coming in eighth overall. They had been as high as third overall on the first lap, but suspension problems dropped them down in the field. Innes Ireland co-drove one of the Cobra roadsters with Masten Gregory at the Targa Florio. Innes recalled the Cobra roadster as "The worst car I ever drove. At the Targa, it was like driving a forty-six-mile-long accident-waiting-to-happen—and sure enough, my co-driver Masten Gregory, put the car and himself over a very steep embankment."

Shelby Invades Europe
From Le Mans to Reims

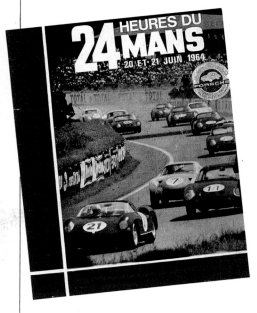

1964 Le Mans program.

24 Hours of Le Mans, 1964
The Gurney/Bondurant Cobra coupe on its finest day. This car finished first in GT and fourth overall, and if it hadn't been for an oil cooler problem that slowed the car considerably, there had been a strong possibility of an overall win.
Eric della Faille/Alexis Callier Collection

12 Hours of Reims, 1964
At Reims, Gurney and Bondurant didn't fare as well. Although the track was well suited to the Cobra coupe, problems set in. Overheating and broken transmissions ended any hope of a victory for both cars. Note the Gurney for President sticker.

Right
Martini Trophy, Silverstone, 1964
Jack Sears driving the famous John Willment Cobra 39PH at Silverstone in 1964. This car had one of the best race win records in Europe.

FERODO FERODO
BRAKE AND CLUTCH LININGS
ON
AVON TY
BOSCH
EXPRESS
39
CASTROL

US **Championship**
Meanwhile, Back on the Home Front....

Riverside USRRC, 1964
Ken Miles on his way to victory in the April 1964 USRRC race at Riverside.

OFFICIAL 50¢ PROGRAM

US ROAD RACING CHAMPIONSHIP
RIVERSIDE INTERNATIONAL RACEWAY
RIVERSIDE, CALIFORNIA

april 25/26 1964

CONDUCTED BY—California Sports Car Club Region of SCCA

1964 USRRC race at Riverside won by Ken Miles.

US Championship
The Racing Explodes

At the Augusta USRRC race in August 1964, we had one of our cherry bomb fights. When we were in the motel, we were shooting M80s into the swimming pool. The things would sink down and explode like a depth charge. All of the people sitting in the restaurant looked out of the window and saw the water erupting out of the pool. They couldn't figure out what the hell was going on.

After the race was over, Dave MacDonald had won another close race with Jim Hall and so the cherry bombs started flying throughout the pits. All of the teams were involved, and the promoter called Shelby and told him to "get your gangsters together and get out of here." All of a sudden I looked down just in time to see a cherry bomb—I think it was thrown by Augie Pabst—land under Shelby's car and explode. With that Shelby just looked at me, laughed, and said, "Let's go." We were all young and having the time of our lives.

Augusta USRRC, August 1964
Dave MacDonald (#97) and Bob Holbert (#98) lead the field off the starting line at Augusta. Jim Hall can be seen in his Chaparral 2 (#66) and Ken Miles in his Cobra (#15). MacDonald won a close race from Hall and Miles won the GT race. It was a short time after this race that the M80s started flying.

USRRC Manufacturer's Championship Trophy won by Shelby American in 1964.

1948
FRANK GRISWOLD
with car second
BRIGGS CUNNINGHAM

1949
MILES COLLIER

1950
ERWIN
GOLDSCHMIDT
AND WIFE

1953 ★ 1957
1959 ★ 1962
WALTER HANSGEN

1954
PHIL WALTERS

1955
SHERWOOD
JOHNSTON

1956 ★ 1961
GEORGE
CONSTANTINE

1958
ED CRAWFORD

1960
AUGIE PABST

1963
BOB HOLBERT

17th ANNUAL
GRAND PRIX SPORTS CAR WEEKEND

Watkins Glen, N.Y.

66

JUNE 26-27
SCCA
Regional Races

JUNE 28
USRRC
1964

OFFICIAL PROGRAM 50 CENTS

FIFTY CENTS

BRIDGEHAMPTON

OFFICIAL PROGRAM

Left
1964 Bridgehampton 500 won by Ken Miles in a Cobra.

Far left
1964 Watkins Glen USRRC won by a Cobra.

119

Road America 500
Ken Miles Drives Two Cobras

Road America 500, 1964
Ken Miles in the Cobra #97 that he co-drove with Skip Scott and John Morton on his way to victory in the Road America 500 in September 1964. Miles finished second overall and first in GT in a repeat of the previous year's results.

Road America 500, 1964
Ken Miles in one of the two Cobras he drove during the 500.

Right
Road America 500, 1964
The Cobra pits at Road America get crowded as Ronnie Bucknum prepares to enter Cobra #98 and Ed Leslie prepares to pull out in #99.

Road America 500, 1964
Ronnie Bucknum takes to the grass at the 1964 Road America 500. This car, which he shared with Ken Miles, DNFed in the race due to a blown engine.

Los Angeles Times GP
Preparing For Race Day

Parnelli Jones won the *Los Angeles Times* Grand Prix at Riverside in his first major sports car race, and the Shelby King Cobra became the first car to score back-to-back wins in this, the most prestigious and richest sports car race in the world.

Right
Los Angeles Times Grand Prix, 1964
The updated 1963 King Cobra to be driven by Ronnie Bucknum was about to be loaded onto the truck for the trip to Riverside and the 1964 *Times* Grand Prix.

Los Angeles Times Grand Prix, 1964
John Collins, Frank Lance, and Ron Butler work on Bob Bondurant's King Cobra on the night before the *Times* Grand Prix at Riverside in 1964. In the background was the car to be driven by Ronnie Bucknum.

Right
Los Angeles Times Grand Prix, 1964
Shelby truck driver Red Pierce lines Ken Miles' Cobra up on the loading ramps prior to loading the car for the 1964 *Times* Grand Prix. Mechanic Red Rose watches.

Los Angeles Times GP
King Cobras Rule—Again

Right
1964 *Times* Grand Prix program.

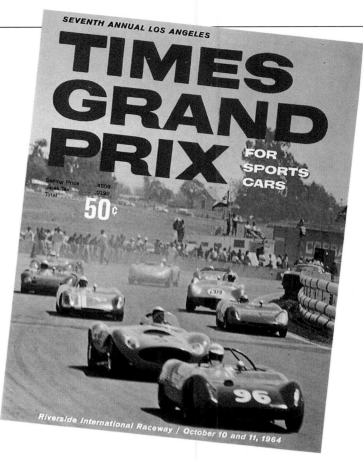

Los Angeles Times Grand Prix, 1964
Bob Bondurant's King Cobra laps Al Unser's Lotus 23 on Bondurant's way to a fifth overall in the 1964 *Times* Grand Prix. Ken Miles drove a 289 Cobra in the race and gave a good account of himself against overwhelming odds until a wheel broke off, ending his bid for a top-ten finish.

Right
Los Angeles Times Grand Prix, 1964
Augie Pabst in the John Mecom Genie (#25) leads Bobby Unser in the Arciero Bros. Lotus 19 Chevy (#96), Ronnie Bucknum in the King Cobra (#95), Parnelli Jones in his King Cobra (#98), Jim Clark in the Lotus 30 (#15), and Richie Ginther in his King Cobra (#92). Jones in the #98 car won the race, giving Shelby American its second consecutive win in the legendary *Times* Grand Prix. This was Jones' first sports car race—and also his first sports car win.

Left
Los Angeles Times Grand Prix, 1964
The start of the 1964 *Times* Grand Prix saw Dan Gurney (#19), Bruce McLaren (#2) eventual winner Parnelli Jones (#94), Jim Clark (#15), Jerry Grant (#8), and Bob Bondurant (#93) lead the strong field towards Turn 1.

Monterey Grand Prix
The King Cobra's Last Race

Luck was not with us at Laguna Seca the following week as Parnelli Jones crashed the King Cobra hard while challenging the leaders. Bob Bondurant finished third behind Dan Gurney and winner Roger Penske.

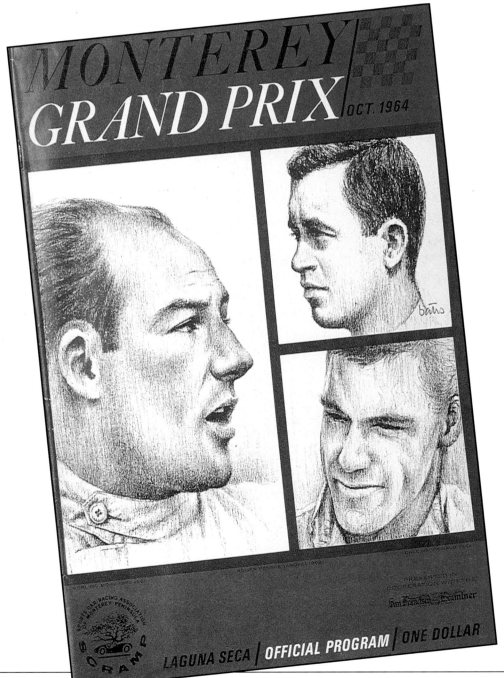

Monterey Grand Prix, 1964
Dan Gurney (#19), Roger Penske (#66), Parnelli Jones (#98), Ronnie Bucknum (#195), Jerry Grant (#8), Bruce McLaren (#47) lead the field away at the start of the Pacific Grand Prix at Laguna Seca in October 1964. Penske in his Chaparral 2 was the winner of the race.

Monterey Grand Prix, 1964
Bob Bondurant is a study in concentration in his King Cobra.

Right
Monterey Grand Prix, 1964
Bob Bondurant in a King Cobra leads Dan Gurney in the Pacesetter Lotus 19B down the famous Laguna Seca Corkscrew during the 1964 running of the Pacific Grand Prix. Bondurant was the fastest-paced King Cobra at this race, finishing third overall while Gurney finished second.

Left
1964 Monterey Grand Prix at Laguna Seca was the last race for the Shelby King Cobras.

Monterey Grand Prix
End of the Road for the King Cobra

Monterey Grand Prix, 1964
Ronnie Bucknum leads Rick Muther's Lotus 23 down the Corkscrew. Bucknum's King Cobra finished fourth overall.

Right
Monterey Grand Prix, 1964
Ronnie Bucknum (#195) leads Bob Bondurant. The positions were reversed at the end with Bondurant finishing third overall and Bucknum finishing fourth overall. This was the last race for the King Cobras in Shelby American colors as the cars were no longer competitive.

Left
Monterey Grand Prix, 1964
Carroll Shelby checks out the wreckage of Parnelli Jones' King Cobra. Jones was challenging for third place when he lost his brakes. Although the car was totalled, Jones escaped with minor injuries.

Shelby's Race Shop
Shelby's New LA Airport Works

In the middle of December 1964, the unsuccessful Ford GT program was handed over to Shelby American, and the two GT40s that raced at Nassau arrived on our door step as a Christmas present. We had a month and a half to make a winner out of this car before the 2,000km race at Daytona.

1965 Shelby American Race Team jacket with name badge. Although this was the official team jacket in 1965, those who still had their blue jackets from 1963 and 1964 favored them.

Right
Shelby American Race Shop, 1965
The new Shelby race shop at the airport facility. In the foreground was the lightweight 390ci Cobra that Ken Miles ran at Nassau, which was now relegated to being a test car. The 427 race car was also being worked on, as were several Ford GTs and GT350 Mustangs. By 1965, the Race Shop was certainly larger and better equipped, but it had lost a lot of its character—and talent.

Daytona Continental
Running Like Clockwork

Daytona Continental, 1965
John Surtees (#77) leads Bob Bondurant (#72), Ken Miles (#73), Walt Hansgen (#88), Allen Grant (#11), Bob Johnson (#12), Jo Schlesser (#13), Rick Muther (#14), and Dan Gurney (#44) at the start of the Daytona race. The Shelby team cars swept the first five positions with Ford GTs in first and third and Cobras in second, fourth, and fifth.

Right
Daytona Continental, 1965
The Shelby coupes undergo last-minute preparation in the garage at Daytona in February 1965. Driver Ed Leslie is sitting in the driver's seat talking to co-driver Allen Grant who is seen by the driver's door. Another driver, John Timanus in the white team jacket, is in the background. The air jacks were new to the Cobra coupes in 1965 and saved considerable time during pit stops.

Daytona Continental
A Shelby American Sweep

The helmet and racing jacket worn by Cobra team driver Allen Grant in 1965.

Right
Daytona Continental, 1965
The Allen Grant/Ed Leslie Cobra coupe heads out of the infield and onto the high banks.

12 Hours of Sebring
The Cobra Coupes Keep On Running

From Daytona, the Shelby race cars were returned to Venice for overhauls and then shipped to Sebring.

The 12 Hours of Sebring provided another GT win for the Cobra coupe with Bob Bondurant and Jo Schlesser finishing fourth overall and first in GT class.

Program for the 1965 Sebring race. Cobra coupes won the GT class.

12 Hours of Sebring, 1965
Carroll Shelby, wired for sound, chats with crew members before the start of the race. Cobra mechanic Jean Stucki is in the background.

Right
12 Hours of Sebring, 1965
One of the most exciting moments in motorsports was the Le Mans start. The start of the 1965 Sebring race shows Shelby's Cobras (#14, #12, #16, and #18) and Ford GT (#11) as well as Dan Gurney's Lotus 19B and two Chaparrals (#3 and #4) leaving the line.

Riverside USRRC
Race Debut of the 427 Cobra

Shelby American would run three Cobras in the USRRC Series and attempt to win a third Manufacturer's Championship in as many years. Most of the USRRC races were run by team cars loaned to drivers like Bob Johnson and Tom Payne.

The first 427 racing Cobra was also completed for Ken Miles to debut at the USRRC Race at Riverside on May 2.

Right
1965 USRRC Riverside championship race.

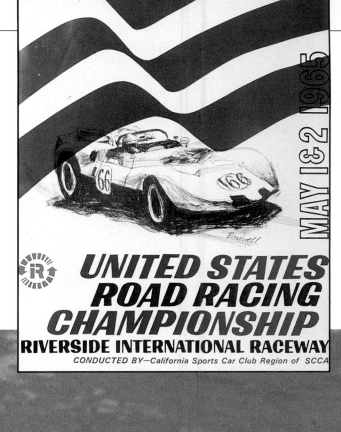

MAY 1&2 1965

UNITED STATES
ROAD RACING
CHAMPIONSHIP
RIVERSIDE INTERNATIONAL RACEWAY
CONDUCTED BY—California Sports Car Club Region of SCCA

Riverside USRRC, 1965
The racing debut of the "real" 427 Cobra was at the Riverside USRRC Race in May 1965. Ken Miles had to run with the Chaparrals and Lola T70s because the car was not yet homologated for the GT class. The car ran well, although it was outclassed.

Laguna Seca USRRC
The Victories Keep Coming

At most of the USRRC races there was no Shelby American Cobra team truck as there had been in the past as there just wasn't the manpower and the priorities had changed. No King Cobras would be run in 1965 since their time had passed and they were not considered competitive.

The Shelby team again swept the boards in the USRRC and won it's third consecutive manufacture's title.

Laguna Seca USRRC, 1965
Ken Miles (#98), Ed Leslie (#96), and Bob Johnson (#97) lead a large field of GT cars away at the start of the June 1965 Laguna Seca USRRC race. This was one of the few real team efforts that Shelby American put up in the series that year.

Upper right
1965 Laguna Seca USRRC race won by Ken Miles.

Lower right
1965 Watkins Glen USRRC won by Bob Johnson's Cobra.

24 Hours of Le Mans
Ford's Downfall

In Europe, Alan Mann's FIA World Championship effort paid off with the Cobras scoring victories at Monza, the Tourist Trophy at Goodwood, Nürburgring, Rossfeld hill climb, Reims, and Enna in Sicily.

Right
Program for 1965 Le Mans.

Below
Programs for the 1965 Tourist Trophy, Spa-Francorchamps, and the Nürburgring. Cobras won at Nürburgring and Oulton Park, but lost at Spa.

Right
24 Hours of Le Mans, 1965
The Thompson/Sears Cobra was the only Ford to finish Le Mans in 1965 and it finished eighth with an oil pickup problem that slowed the car considerably.

Left
24 Hours of Le Mans, 1965
The very fast Grant/Schlesser Cobra ran well among the leaders at Le Mans, but like all the others, dropped out of the race. Defective headbolts were the downfall of the Ford effort that year. *Eric della Faille/Alexis Callier Collection*

World Champions!

First Win For American Cars

The FIA season was wrapped up at Reims, France, on July 4, 1965, and Shelby American became the first American manufacturer to win the World Championship.

Right
Trophy presented to Shelby American by the FIA for winning the World Manufacturer's Championship in 1965.

Below
Reims, 1965
On July 4, 1965, the Shelby American Cobra clinched the World Manufacturer's Championship at Reims. Two Cobra coupes were run that day, one for Bondurant/Schlesser (seen here) and the other for Sears/Whitmore. This was the first championship of its kind ever won by an American car.

Los Angeles Times GP
Back on Home Ground

Right
1965 Cobra Caravan press kit.

Los Angeles Times Grand Prix, 1965
Dick Thompson drove Essex Wire's 427 Cobra at the Times Grand Prix in
1965. Thompson finished well down in the standings in fifteenth place.

On the Canadian Front
Debut of "Gentleman" Tom

Left
Player's 200, Mosport, 1965
When Tom Payne couldn't find his driving suit, he showed up on the Mosport starting grid in a suit and tie. The fans loved it and dubbed him "Gentleman" Tom. Whenever Payne returned to Mosport, he always wore his "specially designed driving suit."

Below
Player's 200, Mosport, 1965
Bob Johnson's Cobra (#33) is seen on the starting grid of the Player's 200 in June 1965. Among those cars on the grid are Jim Hall's Chaparral 2 (#66), Hugh P.K. Dibley's Lola T70 (#5), Walt McKay's Cooper-Ford (#93), Gary Gove's Cheetah (#17), Ludwig Heimrath's McLaren (#1), Chuck Dietrich's Elva-BMW (#57), Wayne Kelly's Porsche Special (#81), and Joe Buzzetta's Elva Porsche (#3). Johnson drove a great race, finishing fourth overall against superior competition.

Canadian Grand Prix, Mosport, 1965
Bob Johnson leads Bruce McLaren (#14) and Lothar
Motschenbacher (#20) during the Canadian Grand Prix in
September 1965. It was getting pretty obvious that the Cobra
was over its head in modified racing by 1965.

Right
Player's 200, Mosport, 1965
"Gentleman" Tom Payne driving his Cobra during the Player's
200 wearing his famous sport coat and tie.

Bonneville Salt Flats
The Last Dash for the Cobra

The Cobra coupe made one last competition appearance and that was at the Bonneville Salt Flats in November 1965. Before it was finished, the Cobra coupe set twenty-three records for flying and standing runs in the National and International Class C category and averaged 170mph for twelve hours.

This was the last appearance of a Cobra in competition under the Shelby American banner.

Bonneville, 1965
The last official act of the Shelby American Cobra team was running a Cobra coupe at Bonneville, Utah, in November 1965. The driving team of Craig Breedlove, Tatersoe, and Tom Greatorex set twenty-three records. *Goodyear*

Postscript
Those Were The Days....

It seemed hard to imagine that the whole factory Cobra racing effort lasted just three years. As John Christy once said, "It's amazing that Shelby played his music as long as he did, and it was great while it lasted; we could have danced all night." And many of us did.

All that remained of the Cobra racing team was to be sold off at the now famous Shelby American fire sale in February 1966.

Shelby American Factory, 1963
A much distributed photograph of Carroll Shelby with the 1963 production 289ci street car and the production race car taken at the Shelby American, Inc., works in Venice California. Those were the days....

Upper and lower right
Invitation and price list for the Shelby American fire sale that was held in February 1966. Among the cars for sale was the "Turd" built by Ken Miles and now fitted with a 427. As Competition Sales Manager Lew Spencer noted in his letter, "Go with the winners for 1966!"

Dear Race Driver:

Shelby American Inc. is happy to announce its Race Assistance Program for 1966 SCCA National Races. This is a new undertaking for us, and we would like to take this opportunity to invite you to participate. Please feel free to contact this department for further information at any time.

You will find enclosed brief specifications of our 427 Cobra and GT-350 Mustang race cars. Included with these is a list of used production and sports racing category cars available at very competitive prices.

Besides cars, Shelby American can provide rebuilt race engines, new race engines, engine development, ZF 5DS-25 transaxle units, Weber 48 IDA carburetors and manifolds for Ford 260-289 engines, and a multitude of other items. Our new Hi-Performance Parts and Accessory Catalog is now available at only 50 cents per copy. Make Shelby American your headquarters for race equipment and preparation.

Also available shortly, FIA Group 1 and Group 2 Ford Mustang sedans, fully race prepared and tested, eligible for the SCCA National Sedan Category, Class "A" and the SCCA Professional Sedan Circuit. Write today for full details and information presently being compiled.

Make a switch, GO WITH THE WINNERS FOR 1966!

Very truly yours,

SHELBY AMERICAN, INC.

Lew Spencer
Competition Sales Manager

LS/lz

USED RACE CARS

3 – Cooper Monacos, less engine and transmission, two assembled, from $3,000.00, one dis-assembled, $2,500.00. Constructed to receive Ford 289 engines and Colotti gearboxes. Reliable, sturdy, can easily win Regional and National races and place well in pro-circuit.

2 – Colotti gearboxes, used, for above, 4 speed - $800.00 each

1 – Colotti gearbox, five speed, brand new - $1,800.00

2 – Cobra 289 race cars, winners of 1965 USRRC Manufacturers' Championship, driven by Bob Johnson and Tom Payne. Fitted with every conceivable option and extra. To be sold "as is" now that season is over. Cars can be fired up and raced right now, but should be thoroughly checked before a serious race program. $6,000.00 each

1 – Cobra 427 race car. Specially prepared for Ken Miles, three races only, every possible option and extra. According to Ken, the best 427 ever built! Fitted dry sump unit for endurance racing - $8,500.00

1 – 427 Modified Special. Constructed by Shelby American Race Department for Ken Miles. Run only at Nassau 1964. Lightweight removable body, Grand National type 427 engine. Can win any Regional and National races and place well in pro-circuit. Car has been rebuilt by Shelby Race Department, presently in primer, will be painted any solid color desired - $6,000.00

1 – Shelby GT-350 Mustang race car. Ex-Jerry Titus Pacific Coast and Daytona Class "B" Championship car. All options and extras fitted - $5,200.00

3 – Cobra Daytona Coupes, team race cars being returned from Europe where they won the World's Manufacturers Championship. Only six of these cars ever constructed. Closed, streamlined coupes, fitted Cobra 289 CID engines and all possible options and extras. Constructed to conform to 1965 FIA Appendix "J" Group 3 Grand Touring regulations. Will comply with 1966 FIA Appendix "J" Group 6 Prototype Sports regulations and SCCA Sports Racing category, Class "C", and be very competitive. Own a "World's Champion" for only $8,700.00.

Prices and specifications subject to change without notice. Prices quoted are F.O.B. Los Angeles, California, but our race vans cover the entire United States and can deliver a car to you for under $350.00.

Index